OVER 200 OF THE WORLD'S MOST FAMOUS RUM RECIPES

DON'T STOP THE
RUM

Yo, Ho, Ho,
and a bottle
of Rum!

RUM

Rum is distilled from sugarcane by-products such as molasses and sugarcane juice. The process of fermentation and distillation produces the distillate, a clear liquid which is aged in oak and other casks. Rum production occurs mainly in the Caribbean.

In the 17th century, the first distillation of rum was produced on Caribbean plantations. By 1664 the American colonies were producing a variety of rums and became the most prosperous industry. English privateers also traded this valuable commodity.

Each island or production area in the Caribbean produces a unique style of rum.

Light rums with a clean taste are traditionally produced in Spanish speaking islands. Rums from Cuba, the Dominican Republic, Panama and Puerto Rico are considered light rums and are widely used in mixed drinks. Light rums, also referred to as light, silver and white rums. They have very little flavor aside from a general sweetness, and are mainly used as a base for cocktails. Light rums are sometimes filtered after aging to remove any color.

Darker rums from English speaking islands are rums with fuller taste containing greater amount of the molasses flavor and a caramel overtone. These rums are mostly from Barbados, Bermuda, Guyana, Jamaica as well as Panama. Also known as black rum, they are a grade darker than gold rum, and generally aged longer in heavily charred barrels. Dark rums have a much stronger flavor than either light or gold rum, and some hints of spices can be detected. The darker color is used to provide substance in rum drinks, as well as color. In addition to uses in mixed drinks, dark rum is the most commonly used in cooking.

Agricultural rums (rhum agricole) are produced in French speaking islands. These rums

2

are made from sugar cane juice and are generally more expensive than molasses based rums, and mostly produced in Guadeloupe, Haiti, Marie-Galante and Martinique, in addition to Trinidad and Panama.

Aguardiente, a spirit distilled from molasses infused with anise, with additional sugarcane juice added after distillation, is produced in Central America and northern South America.

Gold rums, or amber rums, are medium-bodied rums which are generally aged. These gain their dark color from aging in wooden barrels, usually the charred white oak barrels that are the byproduct of Bourbon Whiskey.

Spiced rum obtain their flavor through addition of spices and caramel. Most are darker in color, and based on gold rums. Some are significantly darker, while many cheaper brands are made from inexpensive white rums and darkened with artificial caramel color.

Flavored rums have been infused with flavors of fruits such as coconut, lemon, lime, orange, or mango. These flavor similarly themed tropical drinks which generally comprise less than 40% alcohol, and are also drunk neat or on the rocks.

Overproof rums contain much higher than the standard 40% alcohol. Most of these rums bear greater than 75%, preparations of 151 to 160 proof.

Premium rums are very aged and carefully produced. They have more character and flavor than their "mixing" counterparts, and are generally consumed without the addition of other ingredients.

GLASSES TO USE FOR
DIFFERENT TYPES OF DRINKS

- **14 oz Collins Glass**
  - Soft Drinks
  - Alcoholic Juice Drinks
  - Collins
  - Sours
  - Bloody Mary
- **8 oz Highball**
  - Bourbon/Ginger
  - White Russian
- **4½ oz Rocks**
  - Chilled Shooters
  - Single Shots
- **6 oz Cocktail Glass**
  - Martinis
  - Any chilled "up" drinks
- **8 oz Wine Glass**
  - Wine
  - Champagne

- **2 oz Sherry Glass**
  - Liqueurs
  - Layered Shooters
  - Ports
- **17½ oz Snifter**
  - Brandies
  - Cognacs
- **8½ oz Footed Mug**
  - All Hot Drinks

Always pour light liquors before any liqueurs. Liqueurs are heavier causing the flavor to possibly adhere to the jigger. When pouring numerous drinks, line the glasses up collectively and hold the jigger by the rear of the glass. This allows you to move more quickly and to have better control of the bottle. Always rinse a jigger after using a liqueur. Place the jigger on its side after use in order to allow any excess to drain. When possible, acquire a spill mat: this is a necessity for serious bartenders.

Tulip · Cocktail Glass · Shooter · Irish Coffee Mug · Cordial · Champagne Flute · Wine Goblet

Rocks/Old Fashion · Sherry Glass · Highball Glass · Snifter · Beer Mug · Punch Cup · Daiquiri

Margarita · Martini · Pony · Hurricane · Champagne Saucer · Parfait Glass · Collins

BOTTLE SIZES

Miniature	50 ml	1.7 oz.
Split	187 ml	6.3 oz.
½ Pint	200 ml	6.8 oz.
Tenth	375 ml	12.7 oz.
Pint	500 ml	16.9 oz.
Fifth	750 ml	25.4 oz.
Quart	1 liter	33.8 oz.
Magnum	1.5 L	50.7 oz.
Half Gallon	1.75 L	59.2 oz.
Jeroboam	3 liters	101.4 oz.

MEASUREMENTS

1 Dash	1/32 oz.
1 Teaspoon	1/8 oz.
1 Tablespoon	3/8 oz/
1 Pony	1 oz.
1 Jigger	11/2 oz.
1 Wine Glass	4 oz.
1 Split	6 oz.
1 Cup	8 oz.

STANDARD BAR MEASUREMENTS

Measurements	Metric Equivalent	Standard Equivalent
1 dash	0.9 ml	1/32 oz.
1 teaspoon	3.7 ml	1/8 oz.
1 tablespoon	11.1 ml	3/8 oz.
1 pony	29.5 ml	1 oz.
1 jigger	44.5 ml	1½ oz.
1 miniature	59.2 ml	2 oz.
1 wine glass	119.0 ml	4 oz.
1 split	177.0 ml	6 oz.
1 half pint	257.0 ml	8 oz.
1 tenth	378.88 ml	12.8 oz.
1 "pint" (½ bottle wine)	375.2 ml	12 oz.
1 pint	472.0 ml	16 oz.

DRINK CHART

Number of Drinks in One Hour

Body Weight	1	2	3	4	5	6
100	.038	.075	.113	.150	.188	.225
120	.031	.063	.094	.125	.156	.188
140	.027	.054	.080	.107	.134	.161
160	.023	.047	.070	.094	.17	.141
180	.021	.042	.063	.083	.104	.124
200	.019	.038	.056	.075	.094	.13
220	.017	.034	.051	.068	.085	.102
240	.016	.031	.047	.063	.078	.094

Impaired	Intoxicated
DO NOT DRIVE	DO NOT DRIVE

This is a guide only. Food consumption, medication and other physical conditions may vary these figures.

One drink is one shot of 80 proof liquor, 12 oz. beer, or 4 oz. wine

7

HOW TO STOCK A BAR

- **Spirits**
  - Brandy
  - Gin
  - White or Gold Rum
  - Dark Rum
  - Tequila
  - Vodka (unflavored)
  - Flavored Vodka (orange, lemon, raspberry, etc.)
  - Bourbon Whiskey
  - Tennessee Whiskey
  - Single Malt Whiskey
  - Irish Whiskey

- **Liqueur**
  - Triple Sec or Cointreau
  - Apple Pucker Schnapps (for Appletinis)
  - Kahlua
  - Irish Creme
  - Southern Comfort
  - Amaretto

- **Mixers**
  - Sweet & Sour
  - Lime Juice (Fresh or Roses)
  - Bloody Mary Mix
  - Margarita Mix
  - Fresh Juices (orange, cranberry, pineapple, pomegranate)
  - Club Soda
  - Tonic
  - Ginger Ale
  - Cola
  - Grenadine
  - Cream or Half & Half

- **Garnishes**
  - Lime Wedges
  - Lemon Wedges
  - Orange Slices
  - Maraschino Cherries
  - Olives (regular or stuffed)
  - Cocktails Onions
  - Margarita Salt
  - Sugar

- **Wine and Fortified Wines**
  - Dry Vermouth
  - Sweet Vermouth
  - Red Wine (Cabernet, Merlot, etc.)
  - White Wine (Chardonnay, Sauvignon Blanc, etc.)
  - Sparkling Wine (Champagne, Prosecco, etc.

- **Bitters**
  - Angostura Bitters
  - Campari

THE RECIPIES

Bring Me One Noggin of *Rum,*

won't you, Matey!

ACAPULCO

1½ oz. tequila
½ oz. light rum
½ oz. triple sec

1 oz. sour mix
1 splash lime juice
fresh mint leaves

Shake with ice and strain into an ice filled double old-fashioned glass.
Garnish with mint leaves.

AMERICAN FLYER

1½ oz. light rum
1 Tbsp. lime juice

¼ tsp. sugar
champagne or sparkling wine

Shake first three ingredients together. Strain into chilled glass.
Top with champagne.

AMERICAN PIE

1½ oz. rum
3 oz. lime juice

1½ oz. lemon-lime soda
1 Tbsp. grenadine

Fill a cocktail glass with ice. Pour in rum, lime juice, grenadine.
Top with lemon-lime soda. Stir well.

APPLE COLADA

1 oz. apple schnapps
½ oz. light rum
½ oz. cream of coconut

½ oz. cream
3 oz. pineapple juice
1 maraschino cherry

Combine with crushed ice and blend until smooth.
Garnish with maraschino cherry.

AROUND THE WORLD

1 dash rum
1 dash vodka
1 dash gin
1 dash tequila
1 dash triple sec
1 dash peach schnapps
1 dash Midori
1 dash Blue Curaçao

1 dash 151
1 dash Amaretto-Malibu
1 dash Southern Comfort-Chamord
1 dash sour mix
1 dash orange juice
1 dash pineapple juice
1 dash cranberry juice
1 dash lemon-lime soda

Fill glass with cracked ice. Add alcohol and even parts sour mix,
orange, pineapple, and cranberry juices and lemon-lime soda.
Blend ingredients. Serve in tall glass.

ARUBIAN KISS

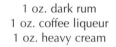

1 oz. vodka	2 dashes Blue Curaçao
¾ oz. rum	1 oz. sour mix
¾ oz. banana liquor	3 oz. pineapple juice

Shake ingredients. Strain into a collins glass with ice.

ATLANTIC DOLPHIN

1 oz. dark rum	1 oz. crème de cacao
1 oz. coffee liqueur	2 crushed Oreo cookies
1 oz. heavy cream	2 oz. milk

Combine and place into a highball glass

BAHAMA MAMA

1½ oz. coconut rum	dash grenadine
1½ oz. dark rum	orange wedge
splash orange juice	maraschino cherry
splash pineapple juice	

Shake over ice. Serve into a hurricane glass.
Garnish with an orange slice and maraschino cherry.

12

BAHAMIAN RAPTURE

¼ oz. coconut rum liqueur   1 oz. dark rum
¼ oz. crème de banana   ½ oz. cream

*Mix dark rum and cream. Pour into glass. Layer remaining in exact
order - crème de banana, coconut rum liqueur.*

BANANA BARBADOS

¾ oz. Barbados rum   splash of sour mix
¾ oz. Jamaican rum   2 scoops vanilla ice cream
½ oz. crème de banana

Blend ingredients. Float a dash of rum. Serve in hurricane glass.

BANANA BOAT

1 oz. rum   1 oz. coffee liqueur
1 oz. cream   1 oz. peppermint schnapps

Layer in exact order into a shot glass.

BANANA DAIQUIRI

1½ oz. rum
1 tsp. triple sec
1½ oz. lime juice

1 tsp. sugar
1 medium banana, sliced

Mix in blender until smooth.

BARBADOS RUM RUNNER

¼ oz. dark rum
½ oz. blackberry brandy
½ oz. banana liqueur

¼ oz. grenadine
½ oz. lime juice

*Blend with ice. Serve in iced champagne glasses
with a swirl of dark rum on top.*

BARBUDA BANANA MAN

1 oz. light rum
¼ oz. lemon juice or lime juice

½ tsp. sugar
1 banana

Blend with ice. Garnish with banana slice.

BARRACUDA

1¼ oz. dark rum
1 oz. pineapple juice
½ oz. lime juice

¼ tsp. sugar
champagne

Shake everything but the champagne. Pour in glass flute.
Top with champagne.

BATIDO DE PIÑA

2½ oz. white rum
5 oz. pineapple

1 tsp. powdered sugar
4 oz. ice

Combine with crushed ice and blend until smooth.

BEACH BUSTER

1 oz. dark rum

2 oz. Sobe Nirvana

Combine in a highball filled with ice. Stir.

BEACHCOMBER

1½ oz. rum
½ oz. triple sec
½ oz. lime juice

dash Maraschino liqueur
lime wedge
fine sugar

Shake with ice. Pour into a chilled cocktail glass with a sugared rim.
Garnish with a lime wedge.

BELLINI

1 oz. pineapple rum
2 oz. sparkling wine
2 oz. peach daiquiri mix

dash Alize
1 tsp. cream of coconut

Blend with crushed ice. Serve in a tulip glass and float with Alize.

BETWEEN THE SHEETS

¾ oz. white rum
¾ oz. brandy

½ oz. triple sec
½ oz. lemon juice

Shake with ice. Strain into glass.

BLACK JAMAICAN

1½ oz. dark rum   ½ oz. coffee liqueur

Combine with ice and stir.

BLACK ORCHID

1 oz. dark rum   ½ oz. grenadine
1 oz. Chambord   ½ oz. lemon-lime soda

Shake with ice. Strain into rocks glass. Top with lemon-lime soda.

BLUE HAWAIIAN

1½ oz. white rum   1 oz. coconut cream
½ oz. Blue Curaçao   ½ cup crushed ice
2 oz. pineapple juice   pineapple slice

Blend. Pour in glass. Garnish with pineapple slice.

BLUE LAGOON

1 oz. rum
½ oz. Blue Curaçao

½ oz. pineapple juice

Pour Rum & pineapple juice over ice in highball.
Float Blue Curaçao.

BLUE MOTORCYCLE

1 oz. rum
1 oz. tequila
1 oz. vodka
1 oz. gin

1 oz. Blue Curaçao
sweet & sour mix
lemon-lime soda
maraschino cherry

Fill a collins glass with ice and add ingredients one by one. Fill with sour
mix and top with of lemon-lime soda. Garnish with maraschino cherry.

BLUE MOUNTAIN

1 ½ oz. spiced rum
1 oz. Blue Curaçao
¾ oz. Tia Maria

¾ oz. vodka
1½ oz. orange juice

Combine with ice and shake. Strain and add ice.

BLUE SKY

1½ oz. Canadian Mist
¾ oz. light rum
¾ oz. Blue Curaçao

8 oz. pineapple juice
10 oz. ice
orange wedge

Blend all ingredients until frozen. Use hurricane glass and garnish with orange slice and umbrella.

BLUEBERRY RUM FIZZ

2½ oz. white rum
½ oz. triple sec
1 Tbsp. lemon juice
1 tsp. blueberry syrup

5 blueberries
splash club soda
1 lemon wedge

*Combine all but soda with ice and shake.
Strain and add soda and ice. Garnish with fruits.*

BOLERO

1½ oz. white rum
¾ oz. apple brandy

¼ tsp. sweet vermouth
lemon twist

*Stir with ice. Strain into a sugar-rimmed cocktail glass.
Garnish with lemon peel.*

BOLO

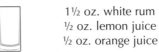

1½ oz. white rum
½ oz. lemon juice
½ oz. orange juice

½ tsp. sugar
orange wedge

Shake with ice. Strain into glass. Garnish with orange wedge.

BONAIRE BOOTY

1 oz. chocolate schnapps
¾ oz. Amaretto

½ oz. gold rum
1 oz. cream

Combine with ice and shake. Strain and serve over ice.

BOOM BOOM PUNCH

1 oz. dark rum
1 Tbsp. orange juice
1 oz. sweet vermouth

3 oz. champagne
banana slices

Mix and pour in a glass. Garnish with banana slices.

BORINQUE

1 tsp. spiced rum
1½ oz. white rum
1 Tbsp. lime juice

½ oz. orange juice
½ oz. passion fruit juice
1 slice orange

Combine with ice and shake. Strain over crushed ice.
Garnish with fruit.

BOSTON SIDECAR

1½ oz. light rum
½ oz. brandy

½ oz. triple sec
½ oz. lemon or lime juice

Combine all the ingredients in a shaker filled with ice.
Shake well and strain into a martini glass.

BRANDY BOAT

2 oz. brandy
1 dash rum
½ oz. club soda
1 tsp. lemon juice
1 slice lemon

1 tsp. pineapple juice
1 tsp. sugar
1 dash lime juice
1 slice orange

Combine all but rum and soda with ice and shake. Strain and add
soda and crushed ice. Float rum on top. Garnish with fruits.

BULL'S MILK

1½ oz. brandy
1 oz. rum
8 oz. milk

1 tsp. powdered sugar
1 dash nutmeg
1 dash cinnamon

Combine with ice and shake. Strain and add ice.
Dust with cinnamon and nutmeg.

BUSHWHACKER

1½ oz. 151 rum
1 oz. Amaretto
2 oz. coffee liqueur
1 oz. crème de cacao

1 oz. Irish Cream
1 oz. vodka
2 oz. pineapple juice
4 oz. coconut cream

Mix in blender with crushed ice. Blend until smooth.

CABLE CAR

1 oz. spiced rum
½ oz. Orange Curaçao

½ oz. lime juice
½ oz. sweet & sour mix

Combine everything in a cocktail shaker with ice. Shake well and
strain into a chilled cocktail glass.

CAFÉ GROG

½ oz. spiced rum
½ oz. brandy
4 oz. coffee

1 tsp. sugar
1 lemon peel

Combine liqueurs with hot coffee and stir. Add sugar as needed.
Garnish with lemon peel.

CALYPSO DAIQUIRI

1¼ oz. spiced rum
2½ oz. sour mix
½ oz. half & half

1 banana
1 tsp. vanilla extract

Blend with ice. Pour into daiquiri glass.

CAPTAIN COOK

1 oz. light rum
¼ oz. Grand Marnier

splash pineapple juice
1 maraschino cherry

Combine with ice and stir. Garnish with maraschino cherry.

CAPTAIN'S COOLER

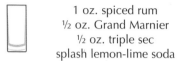

1 oz. spiced rum
½ oz. Grand Marnier
½ oz. triple sec
splash lemon-lime soda

½ oz. cranberry juice
1 oz. orange juice
½ oz. lime juice
lime wedge

Combine all but soda and shake. Strain and add ice.
Fill with soda. Garnish with lime wedge.

CAPTAIN'S MARGARITA

1 oz. spiced rum
½ oz. triple sec
16 oz. frozen limeade

1 cup ice cubes
lime wedge

Blend until smooth. Pour into cocktail glass. Garnish with lime wedge.

CARDINAL SIN PUNCH

1 bottle champagne
1 pint dark rum
8 oz. sweet vermouth
2 quarts claret
1 quart club soda

6 oz. powdered sugar
3 cups lemon juice
6 slices orange
6 slices lemon

Combine all but champagne and soda with ice and stir.
Add ice cubes, club soda and champagne. Serves 12.

CARIBBEAN CRUISE

1 oz. spiced rum
1 oz. dark rum
¾ oz. coffee liqueur
¾ oz. cream of coconut

splash orange juice
splash pineapple juice
lemon twist

Blend with ice. Garnish with a lemon twist.

CARIBBEAN DREAM

½ oz. crème de banana
½ oz. dark rum
½ oz. white crème de cacao

coffee to fill
dash whipped cream

Combine liqueurs and stir. Fill with coffee. Top with whipped cream.

CARIBBEAN HURRICANE

1½ oz. dark rum
1½ oz. white rum
½ oz. grenadine
2 oz. orange juice

2 oz. pineapple juice
½ oz. lime juice
1 tsp. sugar
pineapple wedge

Combine with ice and shake. Strain and add ice.
Garnish with pineapple wedge.

CARIBBEAN SEA

1½ oz. spiced rum
½ oz. Blue Curaçao
1½ oz. coconut cream

3 oz. pineapple juice
pineapple wedge

Mix in blender with ½ cup ice. Blend until smooth.
Garnish with pineapple wedge.

CAYMAN ISLAND RUM FREEZE

2 oz. rum
1 oz. triple sec
1 oz. grapefruit juice
2 oz. orange juice

½ oz. lime juice
½ cup ice cubes
orange wedge

Combine ingredients in blender. Blend until smooth.
Pour into glass. Garnish with orange wedge.

CHAMBORD COLADA

1½ oz. Chambord
1½ oz. rum
2 oz. pineapple juice

½ oz. cream of coconut
¾ oz. ice
pineapple wedge

Place all ingredients in a blender; process on high until smooth.
Garnish with pineapple wedge.

CHAMBORLADA

1 oz. Chambord
½ oz. light rum
½ oz. dark rum

3 oz. pineapple juice
2 oz. cream of coconut
pineapple wedge

Combine all ingredients, except Chambord with ice in blender. Blend.
Pour the Chambord into the bottom of a wine glass. Pour this blended
piña colada mixture on top. Top off with a little more Chambord.
Garnish with pineapple wedge.

CHOCOLATE CREAM

¾ oz. gold rum
¼ oz. dark crème de cacao

¼ oz. white crème de menthe
1 oz. cream

Mix in a shaker or blender with ice. Strain into a cocktail glass.

COCO LOCO

¾ oz. dark rum
¾ oz. coconut rum
½ oz. cream of coconut
½ oz. papaya juice

½ oz. orange juice
½ oz. pineapple juice
¼ oz. grenadine
pineapple wedge

Blend with ice until smooth. Garnish with pineapple wedge.

COCOMOTION

1½ oz. dark rum
4 oz. cream of coconut

2 oz. lime juice
1½ cups ice

Blend with ice and serve in a margarita glass.

COCONUT DAIQUIRI

1 oz. rum
1½ oz. cream of coconut

½ oz. lime juice
1 cup ice

Combine with crushed ice and blend until smooth.

COCONUT PUNCH

1¼ oz. gold rum
2 oz. cream of coconut

½ oz. lemon juice
3-4 Tbsp. vanilla ice cream

*Mix all ingredients in a shaker or blender with crushed ice.
Pour into a tall glass.*

COLLINS

1¼ oz. liquor*
½ Tbsp. powdered sugar

juice of half a lemon
splash club soda

Shake liquor & lemon juice. Pour in Collins glass. Add club soda.

*Tom Collins = gin, Vodka Collins = vodka, Rum Collins = rum,
John Collins = whiskey, usually bourbon.*

COLONIAL TEA PUNCH

1½ oz. brandy
1 oz. spiced rum
1 quart dark tea

12 lemons
12 oz. sugar

*Combine lemon peels, lemon juice, tea, and sugar. Steep for 1-2 hours.
Add liquors and serve hot.   Serves 4.*

COLUMBIA

1½ oz. light rum
½ oz. raspberry schnapps

1 tsp. kirsch
½ oz. lemon juice

Combine with ice and shake. Strain and serve straight up.

29

CONCH SHELL

4 oz. white rum
2 t. lime juice

½ cup ice

Combine with ice and shake. Strain and add ice.

COSMOPOLITANO
The Rum Cosmo

1½ oz. white rum
½ oz. triple sec
¾ oz. cranberry juice

¼ oz. lime juice
lime peel

*Combine all ingredients in cocktail shaker with ice. Shake well. Strain
into a cocktail glass. Garnish with a lime peel.*

CREEPY CRAWLER PUNCH

4 cups of white rum
4 cups of Blue Hawaiian Maui

½ cup Schnapps
1 gallon of orange juice

*Combine ingredients in a large punch bowl with a block of ice in the
center. Dry ice is also good to use for effect. Serves 12.*

CREOLE

2 oz. light rum
1 oz. lemon juice
1 dash Tabasco sauce
1 dash Worcestershire sauce

½ oz. beef bouillon
dash of salt
dash of black pepper
lemon wedge

In a shaker filled with ice, add the rum, beef bouillon, Tabasco, Worcestershire, lemon juice, salt and pepper and shake well. Strain into a highball glass filled with ice and garnish with the lemon wedge.

CREOLE SPLASH

2 oz. spiced rum
3 oz. pineapple juice
3 oz. orange juice

splash of grenadine
orange twist
maraschino cherry

Pour rum into a cocktail glass filled with ice. Fill with pineapple juice and orange juice. Stir and add a splash of grenadine. Garnish with orange twist and maraschino cherry.

CRIMSON TIDE

1½ oz. pineapple rum
1½ oz. white rum

½ oz. grenadine
dash cranberry juice

Build in a collins glass filled with ice. Add rums and grenadine. Fill with cranberry juice.

CROCODILE

½ oz. Blue Curaçao   1 oz. orange juice
½ oz. rum   ½ oz. sour mix
1 dash Orgeat Syrup

Combine with ice and shake. Strain and add ice.

CUBA LIBRE

1¼ oz. rum   dash lime juice
4 oz. cola   lime twist

Blend. Pour in glass over ice. Garnish with lime wedge.

DAIQUIRI

1½ oz. white rum   1 tsp. sugar
juice of 1 lime

Shake with ice. Strain into glass.

DAY IN THE SHADE

1 oz. spiced rum
1 oz. pineapple juice

½ oz. cranberry juice

Shake over ice. Strain into chilled cocktail glass.

DIAMOND HEAD

½ oz. Amaretto
¼ oz. Drambuie
2½ oz. light rum
1 oz. orange juice
1 oz. lime juice

1 oz. grapefruit juice
1 oz. pineapple juice
1 dash grenadine
1 slice pineapple
lime wedge

Combine with ice and shake. Strain and add ice.
Garnish with lime wedge.

DIE HARDER

1½ oz. Blue Curaçao
1½ oz. rum

1½ oz. pineapple juice

Combine with ice and shake. Strain and add ice.

DIRTY ASHTRAY

½ oz. gin
½ oz. vodka
½ oz. light rum
½ oz. tequila
½ oz. Blue Curaçao

½ oz. grenadine
splash pineapple juice
splash sour mix
lemon wedge

Shake, strain into chilled cocktail glass. Garnish with lemon wedge.

DOMINICA BANANA DAIQUIRI

1½ oz. rum
½ oz. crème de banana

½ ripe banana (sliced)
juice of 1 lime

*Blend all ingredients together until smooth
and pour unstrained into a tall chilled glass.*

EGG NOG

3 cups gold rum
1 cup dark rum
2 quarts half & half
1 cup sugar

12 eggs*
4 tsp. vanilla extract
nutmeg

*In a large mixing bowl beat the eggs until light. Add sugar, then the
half & half, rums, and vanilla. Cover and chill over night. Take out of
fridge about ½ hour before serving. Serves 20.*
* Please use caution using raw eggs as it may cause certain illnesses.

EL PRESIDENTE

2 oz. dark rum
4 oz. orange juice
dash of grenadine

maraschino cherry
orange peel

Shake with ice. Strain into cocktail glass.
Garnish with maraschino cherry and orange peel.

ENGLISH CHRISTMAS PUNCH

1 bottle (750ml) dark rum
2 bottles (750ml) dry red wine
3 cups tea

½ cup orange juice
½ cup lemon juice
2 cups sugar

Combine wine, tea and juices in a saucepan. Heat well. Gradually stir
in sugar and rum. Serve warm. Serves about 25.

ERNEST HEMINGWAY

1½ oz. white rum
¼ oz. maraschino liqueur

juice of ½ lime
¼ oz. grapefruit juice

Shake and pour in a glass with crushed ice.

EVERGLADES SPECIAL

1 oz. white rum
1 oz. white crème de cacao

2 tsp. coffee liqueur
1 oz. light cream

Combine with ice and shake. Strain and add ice.

EYE OPENER

1½ oz. light rum
½ oz. triple sec
2 tsp. Pernod

1 tsp. crème de cacao
1 egg yolk*
1 tsp. sugar

*Combine all ingredients in shaker filled with ice. Shake well.
Strain into chilled glass.*

*Please use caution using raw eggs as it may cause certain illnesses.

FISH HOUSE PUNCH

2 quarts rum
1 quart cognac
½ cup peach brandy

1 quart lemon juice
¾ pound sugar

*Dissolve sugar in small amount of water, add lemon juice. Pour
mixture over ice. Add rum, cognac, peach brandy, in exact order.
Let stand for 2 hours, stirring occasionally.*

FROZEN FRUIT DAIQUIRI

1¼ oz. rum
sour mix
½ tsp. sugar

fruit, fruit juice or pureed fruit*
lime wedge

Blend with crushed ice. Garnish with whipped cream & lime edge.

Use lime juice for lime daiquiri, banana for banana daiquiri, pureed strawberries & splash of grenadine for strawberry daiquiri, etc.

GAUGUIN

2 oz. white rum
½ oz. passion fruit syrup
½ oz. lemon juice

¼ oz. lime juice
½ cup crushed ice
maraschino cherry

Blend and pour into chilled glass. Garnish with maraschino cherry.

GEISHA GIRL

1 oz. red rum
1 oz. Midori Melon Liqueur
pineapple juice to fill

pineapple wedge
maraschino cherry

*Combine rum and Midori in a collins glass filled with ice.
Fill with pineapple juice. Garnish with a slice of pineapple
and maraschino cherry.*

GOOMBAY SMASH

1 oz. spiced rum
1 oz. coconut rum
½ oz. crème de banana

splash orange juice
splash pineapple juice

Combine with ice and shake. Blend and serve in hurricane glass.

GREEN BAY SMASH

1 oz. coconut rum
1 oz. Midori
½ oz. crème de banana

splash orange juice
splash pineapple Juice

*Blend all but Midori and pour over ice in tall glass.
Float Midori on top.*

GUAVA COOLER

1½ oz. white rum
½ oz. Maraschino
1½ oz. guava nectar

1 oz. pineapple juice
1 oz. sour mix
¼ tsp. sugar syrup

Combine with ice and shake. Strain and add ice.

HAMMERHEAD

½ oz. spiced rum
½ oz. light rum
½ oz. Malibu
½ oz. vodka

½ oz. grenadine
2 oz. orange juice
1 oz. pineapple juice
pineapple wedge

Combine all but grenadine with ice and stir. Float grenadine on top.
Garnish with a pineapple wedge.

HAVANA BANDANA

2 oz. rum
3 dashes banana liqueur
1 banana

½ oz. lime juice
3 oz. ice

Combine ingredients (except banana liqueur) and blend.
Float banana liqueur on top.

HAVANA COCKTAIL

¾ oz. rum
1¼ oz. pineapple juice

dash lemon juice

Stir with ice. Strain into chilled cocktail glass.

HEAD WIND

1 oz. rum	1 oz. vodka
1 oz. brandy	2 oz. sour mix
½ oz. Blue Curaçao	4 oz. orange juice
1 oz. dark rum	2 oz. pineapple juice
1 oz. light rum	1 pineapple wedge

Combine with ice and shake. Strain and add ice.
Garnish with pineapple wedge.

HEAT WAVE

1 oz. dark rum	6 oz. pineapple juice
1/2 oz. peach schnapps	2 tsp. grenadine

Pour rum and schnapps into a highball glass filled with ice. Add pineapple juice and stir. Float grenadine on top by pouring into the highball glass over the back of a spoon.

HEAVEN

2 scoops vanilla ice cream	dash gin
2 oz. coconut rum	whipped cream
4 oz. orange juice	

Mix in blender. Garnish with whipped cream.

HONOLULU JUICER

1½ oz. Southern Comfort
¼ oz. dark rum
2 oz. pineapple juice
¾ oz. lemon juice

¾ oz. lime juice
1 tsp. powdered sugar
pineapple wedge

Shake and strain into glass over ice. Garnish with pineapple wedge.

HORNY GOAT

2 oz. lime flavor rum
lemon-lime soda

splash cranberry juice

Fill glass with ice. Add rum, them fill with lemon-lime soda,
leaving a little room. Top with splash of cranberry juice.

HOT BUTTERED RUM

2 oz. rum
apple cider
1 lemon twist

1 cinnamon stick
1 clove
1 tsp. of butter

Heat apple cider. In a mug add spices and rum.
Fill with hot cider & float butter on top.

HOT RUMBA

2 oz. gold rum
hot chocolate

3-4 little marshmallows

In a glass mug add rum and fill with hot chocolate. (If using instant follow the directions on the box). Garnish with little marshmallows or marshmallow cream.

HURRICANE

1 oz. rum
1 oz. dark rum
1 oz. apricot brandy

splash grenadine
2 tsp. lime juice
lime wedge

*Shake with ice. Serve in hurricane glass.
Garnish with lime wedge.*

ICED RUM COFFEE

1½ oz. white rum
1 tsp. spiced rum
6 oz. coffee

1 tsp. sugar
2 Tbsp. whipped cream

*Combine rums, iced coffee and sugar. Fill glass with ice.
Top with whipped cream.*

ISLAMORADA CHAMPAGNE COCKTAIL

1 oz. rum
3 oz. champagne
1 tsp. sugar

dash bitters
strawberry

In a tall glass mix rum, sugar and bitters. Fill with champagne.
Garnish with strawberry.

ISLAND BREEZE

2 oz. coconut flavored rum
1 oz. grenadine

pineapple juice to fill
pineapple wedge

In a highball glass filled with ice, pour rum and grenadine.
Top with pineapple juice. Stir well. Garnish with a pineapple wedge.

ISLAND ICED TEA

½ oz. rum
½ oz. dark rum
1 oz. light rum
dash 151 rum
1 tsp. Falernum

2 dashes lemon juice
1 cup tea
1 lemon twist
1 sprig mint

Combine all but 151 Rum with ice. Shake. Strain and add ice.
Float 151 rum on top. Garnish with lemon and mint.

ISLE OF COCONUT

1½ oz. white rum
2 tsp. cream of coconut
2 tsp. lime juice
1 tsp. orange juice

½ tsp. sugar
1 tsp. lemon juice
coconut shavings

Mix all in blender with 3 oz. crushed ice until smooth.
Garnish with coconut.

ISLE OF PINES

1½ oz. light rum
1 tsp. peppermint schnapps
½ oz. lime juice

mint leaves
3 oz. ice

Combine all ingredients except leaves. Blend. Pour in cocktail glass.
Garnish with mint leaves.

ITALIAN PECKER

¼ oz. spiced rum,
¼ oz. Galliano
¼ oz. cream

¼ oz. Tuaca
½ oz. Mozart

Shake with ice. Strain into shot glass.

JAMAICA GINGER

2 tsp. 151 rum
½ oz. Jamaican rum
1½ oz. white rum
2 tsp. Falernum
2 tsp. lime juice

1 tsp. white crème de menthe
splash ginger beer
1 slice pineapple
1 chunk ginger

Combine rums, Falenum and juice with ice. Shake. Strain and add ice. Fill with ginger beer. Dip pineapple in white crème de menthe. Garnish with pineapple slice and ginger.

JAMAICA GLOW

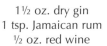

1½ oz. dry gin
1 tsp. Jamaican rum
½ oz. red wine

2 tsp. orange juice
lemon wedge

*Combine with ice. Shake. Strain over crushed ice.
Garnish with lemon wedge.*

JAMAICA ME CRAZY

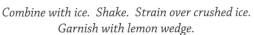

1½ oz. dry gin
1 tsp. Jamaican rum
½ oz. red wine

2 tsp. orange juice
lemon wedge

*Combine with ice. Shake. Strain over crushed ice.
Garnish with lemon wedge.*

JAMAICAN BANANA

½ oz. light rum
½ oz crème de banana
½ oz. white crème de cacao

½ oz. cream
2 scoops vanilla ice cream
banana slice

Mix in blender until smooth. Garnish with banana slice.

JAMAICAN COFFEE

1 oz. coffee liqueur
¾ oz. rum
coffee to fill

whipped cream
maraschino cherry

Pour coffee over coffee liqueur and rum in mug.
Top with whipped cream. Garnish with maraschino cherry.

JAMAICAN EGG CREAM

1 oz. gin
1½ oz. Jamaican rum
1 tsp. lemon juice

1 oz. light cream
½ tsp. sugar
dash club soda

Combine all but soda with ice. Shake. Strain and add soda and ice.

JOLLY ROGER

1 oz. Drambuie   dash club soda
1 oz. light rum   ½ oz. lime juice
3 dashes Scotch

Combine all but soda with ice. Shake. Strain and add soda and ice.

KAHUNA

1 oz. dark rum   ¾ oz. lime juice
1 oz. spiced rum   ¾ oz. pineapple juice
1 oz. light rum   ½ tsp. sugar
½ oz. 151 rum   1 wedge pineapple
½ oz. apricot liqueur   1 maraschino cherry

Combine all but 151 rum with ice. Shake. Strain and add ice.
Float 151 rum on top. Garnish with fruit.

KAHUNA BANANA

1½ oz. coffee liqueur   2 oz. cream of coconut
¾ oz. rum   1 cup ice
2 oz. pineapple juice   1 banana

Blend together. Garnish with banana slice.

KALANI BOY

1 oz. light rum
1 oz. dark rum
½ oz. 151 rum
½ oz. guava juice
¼ oz. grenadine

1 oz. lemon juice
½ oz. orange juice
½ oz. passion fruit juice
½ oz. pineapple juice
pineapple wedge

Combine all but 151 rum with ice. Shake. Strain and add crushed ice.
Float 151 rum on top. Garnish with pineapple wedge.

KEY LARGO

2 oz. rum
1 oz. grapefruit juice
juice of 1 lime

1 tsp. powdered sugar
dash of bitters
lime twist

Shake with ice. Strain into cocktail glass. Garnish with lime twist.

KEY WASTED

1 oz. spiced
¼ oz. Cointreau

juice of 1 lime

Shake with ice. Strain into chilled cocktail glass.

LADY IN BED

1½ oz. spiced rum   2 oz. fresh strawberries
1½ oz. Irish Cream   ¾ cup crushed ice
2 oz. coconut cream   strawberry

Blend until smooth. Pour into a chilled collins glass.
Garnish with a strawberry.

LAVA FLOW

1 oz. light rum   ½ oz. lemon juice
1 oz. spiced rum   1 slice lemon
1 dash Orange Curaçao   4 oz. ice
1 dash grenadine   pineapple wedge
1½ oz. pineapple juice

Combine with crushed ice. Blend until smooth.
Garnish with a pineapple wedge.

LEEWARD

2 tsp. sweet vermouth   2 tsp. Calvados
1½ oz. white rum   lemon twist

Combine with ice. Shake. Strain and add ice.
Garnish with lemon twist.

LETHAL INJECTION

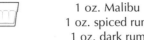

1 oz. Malibu
1 oz. spiced rum
1 oz. dark rum
1 oz. Crème de Noyaux

splash orange juice
splash pineapple juice
pineapple wedge

Shake with ice. Strain into chilled rocks glass.
Garnish with pineapple wedge.

LIBERTY COCKTAIL

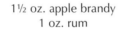

1½ oz. apple brandy
1 oz. rum

½ tsp. sugar
apple wedge

Combine with ice. Shake. Strain into chilled cocktail glass.
Garnish with apple wedge

LIFESAVER

1 oz. coconut flavored rum
1 oz. melon liqueur

2 oz. pineapple juice
maraschino cherry

Combine ingredients with ice. Swirl lightly and strain into a chilled
cocktail glass. Garnish with a maraschino cherry.

LIMBO

2 oz. white rum
1½ oz. crème de banana

1 oz. orange juice
banana slice

*Combine all ingredients in cocktail shaker with ice. Strain into
a chilled cocktail glass. Garnish with banana slice.*

LIME DAIQUIRI FREEZE

1½ oz. rum
1 oz. lime juice
4 oz. sour mix

1½ cups crushed ice
lime wedge

*Blend until smooth. Pour into a hurricane glass.
Garnish with a lime wedge.*

LIMEY

2 oz. light rum
1 oz. lime liqueur
½ oz. triple sec

1 tsp. lime juice
1 cup crushed ice
lime twist

*Blend ingredients except lime twist in a blender filled with 1 cup ice.
Pour into a chilled red wine glass. Garnish with the lime twist.*

LITTLE DEVIL COCKTAIL

1 oz. lemon juice 3/4 oz. gin
3/4 oz. rum dash triple sec

Shake with ice. Strain into chilled cocktail glass.

LITTLE PRINCESS COCKTAIL

1 1/4 oz. rum 1 1/4 oz. sweet vermouth

Stir with ice. Strain into chilled cocktail glass.

LONG BEACH ICED TEA

1/2 oz. vodka 1/2 oz. sweet & sour
1/2 oz. gin 1 oz. cranberry juice
1/2 oz. rum dash lemon lime soda
1/2 oz. tequila lemon twist
1/2 oz. triple sec

Combine ingredients in a cocktail glass with ice.
Garnish with lemon twist.

LONG ISLAND ICED TEA

¾ oz. rum
¾ oz. gin
¾ oz. vodka
¾ oz. tequila

¾ oz. triple sec
¾ oz. sour mix
splash of cola
lemon wedge

Shake liquors with sour mix. Pour in hurricane glass. Add splash of cola. Garnish with a lemon wedge.

LUCKY LADY

¾ oz. light rum
¼ oz. anisette
¼ oz. white crème de cacao

¾ oz. cream
1 cup ice

Blend ingredients with ice. Pour into a margarita glass.

MAI TAI

2 oz. light rum
1 oz. triple sec
dash of high-proof dark rum
1 tsp. almond-flavored syrup
1 tsp. grenadine

1 tsp. lime juice
½ tsp. powdered sugar
pineapple wedge
maraschino cherry

Shake with ice. Strain into tall glass about ¼ full with crushed ice. Top with a dash of high-proof dark rum. Garnish with cherry and pineapple wedge.

MALIBU

¾ oz. spiced rum   orange juice
¾ oz. vodka

Build over ice in highball glass.

MALIBU ITALIAN SURFER

1 oz. spiced rum   splash cranberry
½ oz. Amaretto   splash pineapple juice

Build over ice in highball glass.

MALIBU ORANGE COLADA

1½ oz. spiced rum   2 oz. cream of coconut
1 oz. triple sec   pineapple wedge
2 oz. pineapple juice

Blend with ice until smooth. Garnish with pineapple wedge.

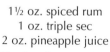

MAMA'S MARTINI

1 oz. spiced rum
1 oz. coffee liqueur

1 oz. icy cold milk
chocolate shavings

Shake well and serve "up" in a martini glass. Garnish with chocolate.

MANGO DAIQUIRI

1½ oz. light rum
1 Tbsp. triple sec
1½ oz lime juice

1 tsp. sugar
2 oz. pureed mango
½ cup crushed ice

Blend with 1 cup crushed ice. Pour in glass.

MARATHON SPARKLER

1 oz. spiced rum
1 oz. ruby red grapefruit juice
champagne

dash of grenadine
strawberry

Fill glass with chilled champagne. Shake rum, grapefruit juice and grenadine with ice. Strain into a champagne flute. Garnish with strawberry on the rim.

MARTINIQUE PUNCH

2 oz. rum
2 oz. mango
2 oz. orange juice

lime wedge
1 tsp. sugar
½ cup ice

Stir. Serve on rocks glass.

MAUI FIZZ

1½ oz. light rum
1 slice pineapple
1 oz. lemon juice

2 tsp. sugar
1 egg* (optional)
1 cup ice

Blend ingredients with ice. Mix well. Pour into a cocktail glass.
*Please use caution using raw eggs as it may cause certain illnesses.

MAUNA KEA MARTINI

1½ oz. gold rum
½ oz. macadamia nut liqueur

¼ oz. chocolate liqueur
½ oz. cream

*Combine in a mixing glass with ice. Stir gently and strain
into a chilled cocktail glass.*

MIAMI RUM YUM

1 oz. Irish Cream   1 oz. cream or milk
1 oz. rum

Blend with ice. Pour in chilled cocktail glass.

MOJITO

2 oz. white rum   ½ tsp. powdered sugar
splash of club soda   mint leaves

Muddle mint leaves with powdered sugar. Add ice, rum and top with club soda. Garnish with a sprig of fresh mint.

MONKEY FIZZ

1 oz. coconut rum   2 oz. pineapple juice
1 oz. melon liqueur   ½ oz. lemon juice
½ oz. crème de banana   club soda
2 oz. orange juice

Combine all ingredients except club soda in shaker with ice. Shake well and strain into glass filled with fresh ice. Top with a splash of club soda.

MONTEGO MARGARITA

1½ oz. rum   1 oz. lime juice
½ oz. triple sec   1 cup crushed ice

Blend with ice and serve.

MULATTA

2 oz. white rum   juice of ½ lime
¼ oz. brown crème de cacao   1 cup crushed ice

Blend with ice. Strain into ¼ ice filled cocktail glass.

NEUTRON BOMB

1 oz. beer   ¼ oz. Amaretto
¼ oz. vodka   ¼ oz. Sloe Gin
¼ oz. rum   ¼ oz. Galliano
¼ oz. triple sec   splash orange juice

Shake with ice. Strain into chilled cocktail glass.

NIRVANA

1½ oz. dark rum   ½ tsp. sugar
½ oz. grenadine   grapefruit juice

Combine rum, grenadine and sugar in a shaker filled with ice.
Shake and strain into a chilled collins glass filled with ice.
Top with grapefruit juice and stir gently.

NUDE BEACH

1 oz. gold rum   ½ oz. grenadine
2 oz. pineapple juice   dash lime juice
2 oz. orange juice   lime wedge

Combine all ingredients in a shaker with ice. Mix well and strain
into a chilled collins glass filled with crushed ice.
Garnish with a lime wedge.

NUTTY JAMAICAN

1 oz. spiced rum cream   ½ oz. Frangelico

Hand swirl liquors over ice. Strain into glass.

NYMPHOMANIAC

1 oz. spiced rum
¼ oz. peach schnapps

¼ oz. spiced rum

Shake. Swirl into glass.

OUTRIGGER

1 oz. light rum
½ oz. rum
½ oz. Amaretto

splash of cranberry juice
splash pineapple juice
orange slice

Shake. Strain into chilled cocktail glass. Float rum on top.
Garnish with orange slice.

PATRIA COLADA

1 oz. gold rum
1 oz. coconut milk
1 oz. concentrated passion fruit (maracuja) juice

shaved coconut
chopped mango

Blend passion fruit juice and coconut milk with 2 cups crushed ice.
Pour into glass and float rum on top. Garnish with shaved coconut
and chopped mango.

PEACH COLADA

1¼ oz. rum
2 oz. peach slices with syrup

1 oz. cream of coconut
1 oz. pineapple juice

Blend and pour into cocktail glass. Garnish with peach slice.

PEARL NECKLACE

1 oz. vodka
1 oz. white crème de cacao

splash of cream

Shake with ice. Strain into chilled cocktail glass.

PIÑA COLADA

2 oz light rum
3 Tbsp. cream of coconut

3 Tbsp. pineapple juice
pineapple wedge

Shake with ice. Serve in hurricane glass. Or blend with ice cream for frozen variation. Garnish with fresh pineapple wedge. Top with whipped cream if frozen.

PINEAPPLE FIZZ

2 oz. rum
1 oz. pineapple juice

½ Tbsp. powdered sugar
club soda to fill

Shake with ice. Pour into cocktail glass and fill with club soda.

PINK LEMONADE

1 oz. lime rum
¾ oz. triple sec
splash of sour mix

cranberry juice
lime soda

Shake over ice. Serve up or on the rocks.

PINK PANTHER

1¼ oz. light rum
¾ oz lemon juice
¾ oz. cream

½ oz. grenadine
maraschino cherry

*Mix in a shaker or blender with ice and strain into a cocktail glass.
Garnish with maraschino cherry.*

PLANTERS PUNCH

1½ oz. rum
¾ oz. triple sec
splash dark rum
splash of sour mix

2 oz. pineapple juice
2 oz. orange juice
dash of grenadine

*Shake. Pour over ice in hurricane glass. Float dark rum on top.
Garnish with orange slice.*

PUERTO RICAN RUMBALL

1 oz. rum
¾ oz. Midori

splash orange juice

Shake with ice. Strain into chilled cocktail glass.

QUARTER DECK COCKTAIL

1½ oz. rum
splash of dry sherry

lime juice

Stir over ice. Strain into chilled cocktail glass.

RAIN FOREST

1 oz. white rum
1 oz. melon liqueur
1 t. cream of coconut

1 oz. passion fruit
1 cup crushed ice

Blend until smooth. Pour into a tall glass.

RASPBERRY ICED TEA

½ oz. gin
½ oz. vodka
½ oz. light rum

½ oz. tequila
½ oz. Chambord
splash sour mix

Shake. Strain into chilled cocktail glass or serve on the rocks.
Float ½ oz. Chambord.

RUM FIZZ

2 oz. white rum
¾ oz. lemon juice
1 tsp. sugar

club soda to fill
¼ cup ice

Shake white rum lemon juice and sugar. Pour in glass with ice.
Fill with club soda.

RUM HIGHBALL

2 oz. white or dark rum   lemon peel
ginger ale to fill

Pour rum into a glass over ice. Fill with ginger ale.
Garnish with lemon peel.

RUM PUNCH

1 oz. dark rum   1 dash grenadine
1 oz. white rum   lemon slice
1 oz. gold rum   orange slice
2 oz. orange juice   pineapple wedge
2 oz. pineapple juice   maraschino cherry
juice of ½ lime

Shake rum and juices with ice. Top with grenadine.
Garnish with fruit.

RUM RICKEY

1½ oz. light rum   club soda to fill
½ lime

Pour rum into highball glass with ½ filled with ice. Squeeze lime
and drop into glass. Fill with club soda and stir.

RUM TOM COLLINS

2 oz. rum
1 oz. lemon juice
1 tsp. superfine sugar

3 oz. club soda
maraschino cherry
orange slice

Combine rum, lemon juice and sugar in a shaker half-filled with ice cubes.
Strain into cocktail glass filled with ice cubes.
Add club soda. Garnish with maraschino cherry.

SAINT JOHN CITRUS COOLER

2 oz. white rum
½ oz. triple sec
1 oz. orange juice
½ oz. fresh lime juice

1 tsp. sugar
lemon-lime soda
lemon wedge
lime wedge

Shake all but soda with ice. Strain over ice into glass. Fill with soda and
stir. Garnish with lemon and lime wedges.

SAINT THOMAS RUM COCKTAIL

1½ oz. white or gold rum
½ oz. lime juice

1 tsp. grenadine

Shake with ice. Strain over ice into glass.

SANTIAGO

1½ oz. white rum
juice of 1 lime
¼ oz. grenadine

1 tsp. sugar
lime peel

Shake with ice. Pour into cocktail glass.
Garnish with lime peel.

SCOOBY SNACK

1 oz. Midori
1 oz. spiced rum

splash of pineapple juice
splash of half & half

Shake all ingredients with ice. Pour into tumbler.

SCORPION

1 oz. dark rum
1 oz. white rum
1 oz. brandy

1 oz. triple sec
3 oz. pineapple juice
dash of grenadine

Shake all ingredients with ice. Serve over ice in highball glass.

SEX WITH AN ALLIGATOR

1 oz. Midori
1 oz. spiced rum
pineapple juice

splash Chambord
splash Jagermeister

*Shake and strain into chilled cocktail glass. Drop a drizzle of Chambord &
let fall to the bottom. Float a thin layer of Jagermeister on top.*

SIMPLY BONKERS

1 oz. Chambord
1 oz. rum

1 oz. cream

Shake with ice. Strain into rocks glass.

SMOOTH SCREW

½ oz. coffee liqueur
½ oz. spiced rum

1½ oz. pineapple juice

*Shake coffee liqueur and pineapple juice with ice.
Pour into cocktail glass. Float rum on top.*

SOUTH SEA

1½ oz. white rum   ¾ oz. lime juice
¾ oz. Blue Curaçao

Shake with ice. Strain into cocktail glass.

SPANISH COFFEE

½ oz. coffee liqueur   whipped cream
½ oz. rum   maraschino cherry
coffee

Build in coffee mug. Top with whipped cream.
Garnish with maraschino cherry.

STORM CLOUD

1 oz. coffee liqueur   2 drops cream
½ oz. 151 rum

Swirl over ice. Strain into shot glass.
Drop cream in shot using a straw.

STRAWBERRY BANANA RUM DUMB

2 oz. rum
2 oz. strawberry puree
1 oz. orange juice
1 oz. pineapple juice

4 oz. ice
2 oz. whipped cream
1 fresh banana

Blend until smooth. Pour into a hurricane glass.
Top with more whipped cream.

STRAWBERRY COLADA

1¼ oz. rum
2 oz. frozen strawberries
1 oz. cream of coconut
1 oz. pineapple juice

½ cup crushed ice
maraschino cherry
pineapple wedge

Blend rum and juices with ice until smooth.
Garnish with maraschino cherry and pineapple wedge.

STRAWBERRY DAIQUIRI

1½ oz. rum
4 oz. fresh strawberries
splash sour mix

dash grenadine
dash whipped cream

Blend with crushed ice. Garnish with whipped cream.

STRAWBERRY SMASH

1 oz. light rum
1 oz. wildberry schnapps
½ oz. 151 rum

1 oz. sour mix
1 cup strawberries
1 banana

Blend with crushed ice. Serve in hurricane glass.
Garnish with fresh fruit.

TIA RUMBA

2 oz. coffee liqueur
2 oz. rum

coffee bean

Shake over ice. Strain into chilled cocktail glass.
Garnish with coffee bean.

TIDAL WAVE

1 oz. 151 rum
1 oz. spiced rum
1 oz. vodka

splash sour mix
splash cranberry juice

Shake over ice. Strain into shot glass.

TOBAGO TEA

½ oz. tequila
½ oz. vodka
½ oz. rum
½ oz. Jim Beam

½ oz. Blue Curaçao
¼ oz. sweet & sour mix
1 oz. cola
lime wedge

Shake over ice. Strain into cocktail glass. Garnish with lime wedge.

TRINIDAD GRASSHOPPER

1 oz. light rum
¼ oz. green crème de menthe

½ oz. cream

Mix in shaker or blender with ice and strain into cocktail glass.

TROPICAL STORM

1 oz. light rum
½ oz. banana liqueur
2 oz. orange juice
1 splash grenadine

1 splash pineapple juice
½ cup crushed ice
1 sliced banana

Blend until smooth. Pour into hurricane glass.

URINE SAMPLE

1 oz. spiced rum
1 oz. Amaretto

1 oz. orange juice
1 oz. pineapple juice

Hand swirl over ice. Strain into rocks glass.

VAN VLEET

3 oz. rum
1 oz. maple syrup

1 oz. lemon juice

Shake over ice. Pour in cocktail glass.

VESUVIO

1 oz. light rum

½ oz. sweet vermouth

Shake with ice to serve on the rocks or strain to serve straight up.

VETERAN

2 oz. dark rum   ½ cherry brandy

Serve in old-fashioned glass with ice.

VICIOUS SID

1½ oz. light rum   1 oz. lemon juice
½ oz. Southern Comfort   1 dash bitters
½ oz. triple sec

Shake. Serve in an old-fashioned glass.

VIRGIN ISLANDS RUM RUNNER

1 oz. rum   splash orange juice
½ oz. blackberry brandy   dash grenadine
1 oz. crème de banana   dash dark rum
splash pineapple juice

Shake. Serve on the rocks in highball glass.
Float a bit of dark rum on top.

VOODOO SHOOTER

1 oz. 151 rum
1 oz. coffee liqueur

1 oz. spiced rum
1 oz. cream

Serve in old-fashioned glass with ice.

WEST INDIAN PUNCH

2 oz. dark rum
¾ oz. banana liqueur
1 oz. pineapple juice

1 oz. orange juice
juice of ½ lime
nutmeg

Shake with ice. Strain into cocktail glass over ice.
Sprinkle with nutmeg.

WHITE LION

½ oz. light rum
juice of ½ lemon
½ t. grenadine

1 tsp. powdered sugar
2 dashes bitters

Blend with ice. Strain to serve up in chilled cocktail glass.

WHITE SANDS

1 oz. vodka
½ oz. coconut rum
splash triple sec

1 scoop vanilla ice cream
1 cup crushed Ice

Blend until smooth. Pour into a collins glass.

WITCHES BREW

1¼ oz. spiced rum
¾ oz. white crème de cacao
¼ oz. grapefruit juice

¾ oz. orange juice
2 gummy worms

Shake and serve into martini glass. Garnish with gummy worms.

XYZ

1 oz. rum
½ oz. triple sec

splash sour mix

Shake over ice. Strain. Serve up in chilled cocktail glass.

YELLOW BIRD

1 oz. rum
1 oz. Galliano
1 oz. crème de banana

splash orange juice
splash pineapple juice
dash of lime juice

Blend with ice. Pour into cocktail glass.

YELLOW SUBMARINE

1½ oz. rum
1 oz. Orange Curaçao

splash sour mix

Shake with ice. Pour into cocktail glass.

YO HO HO AND A BARREL OF RUM

1½ oz old-fashioned root beer schnapps
1 oz. rum

1 oz. milk or cream

Combine in blender with ice until smooth.

Z STREET SLAMMER

1¼ oz. spiced rum
¾ oz. crème de banana

¾ oz. pineapple juice
¼ oz. grenadine

Shake with ice. Strain into rocks glass.

ZOMBIE

¾ oz. light rum
¾ oz. dark rum
¾ oz. gold rum
1 oz. lemon juice

½ tsp. sugar
½ oz. cherry brandy
maraschino cherry

Blend the rums and lemon juice together with ice.
Strain into collins glass. Garnish with maraschino cherry.

INDEX

INDEX